This Book Belongs to:

Welcome to the start of the journey where you will learn to draw the world of Minecraft! We will start from the simple most easy forms moving towards more complex characters! Here are presented the few tools you will need to accomplish great results... no worries it is nothing special only things that lay around the house! Yay! Can't wait to start!

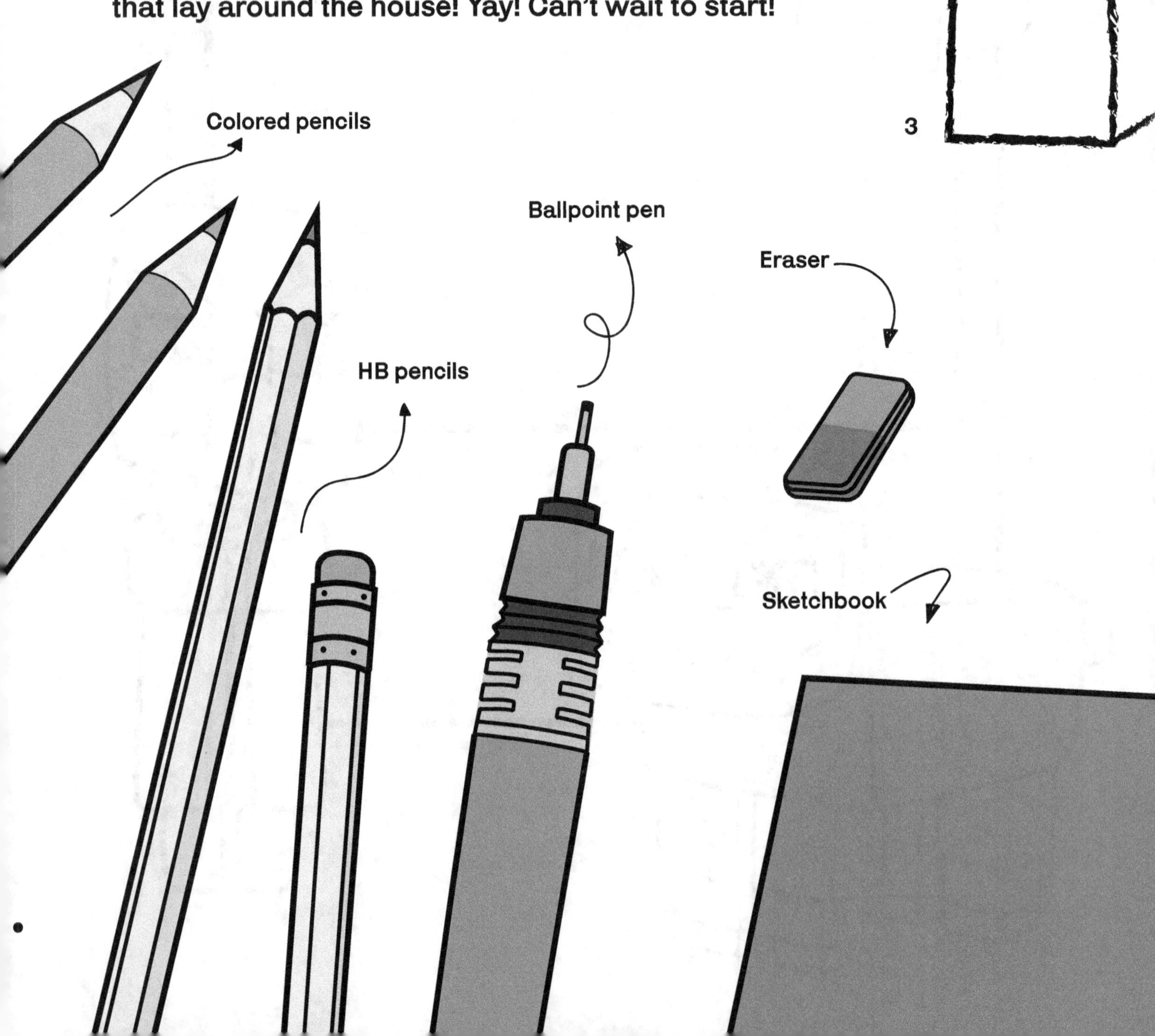

HOW TO DRAW
FOR
MINECRAFTERS

CUBE HUNTER

Rock Cooper

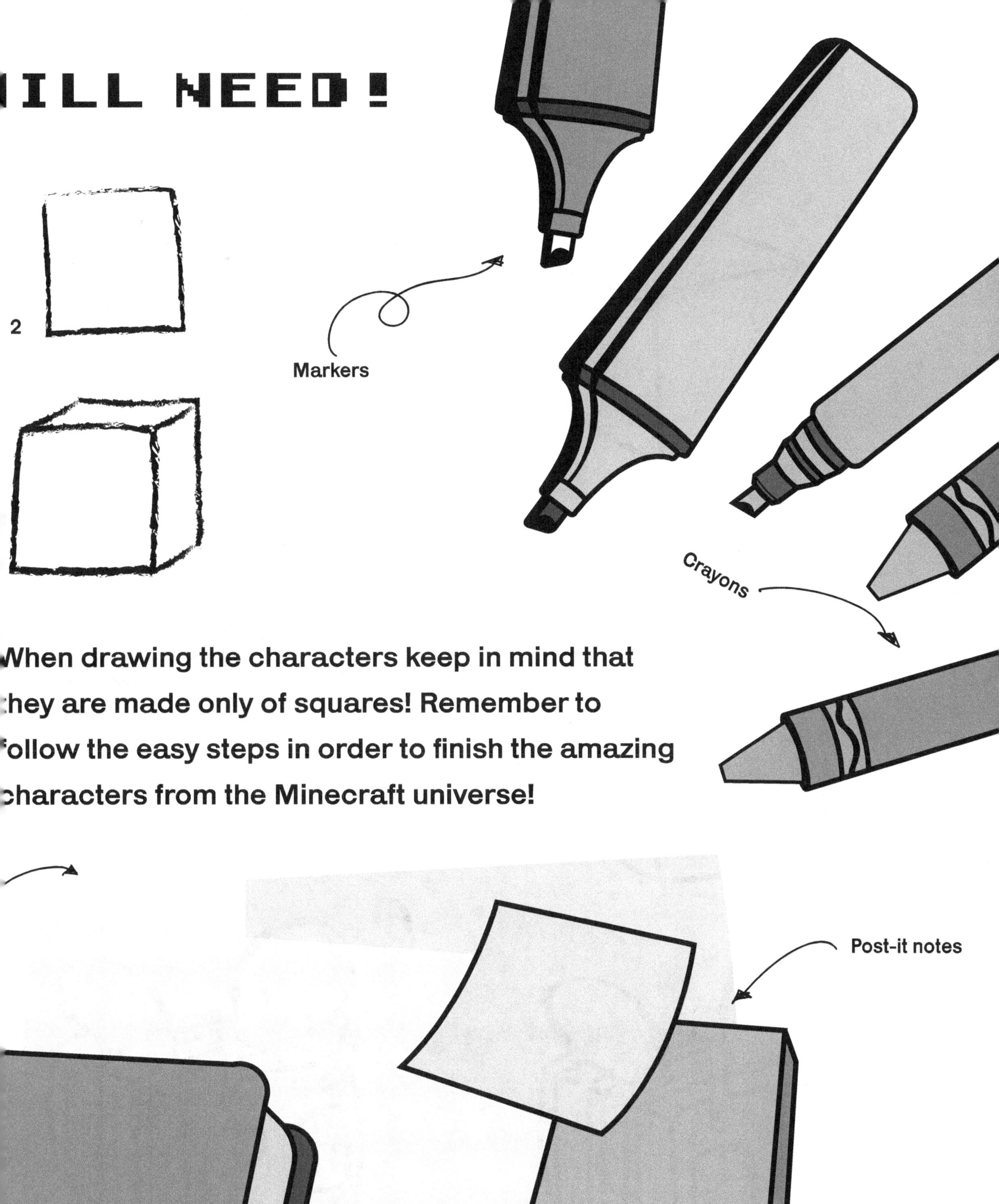

When drawing the characters keep in mind that they are made only of squares! Remember to follow the easy steps in order to finish the amazing characters from the Minecraft universe!

BEE

1

2

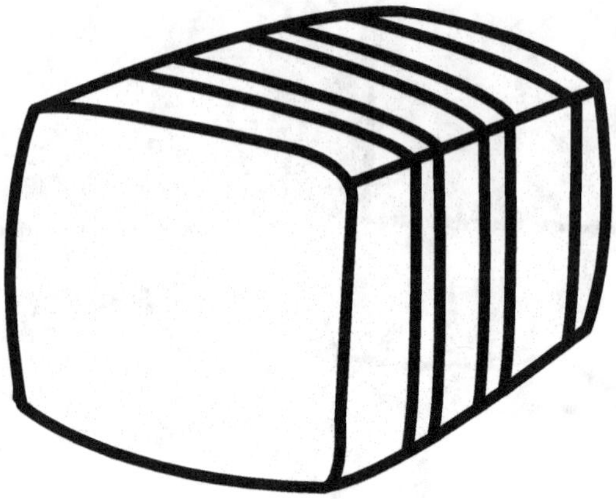

3

4

5

6

Now, it's your turn

SPIDER

1

2

3

4

5

6

Now, it's your turn

SKELETON

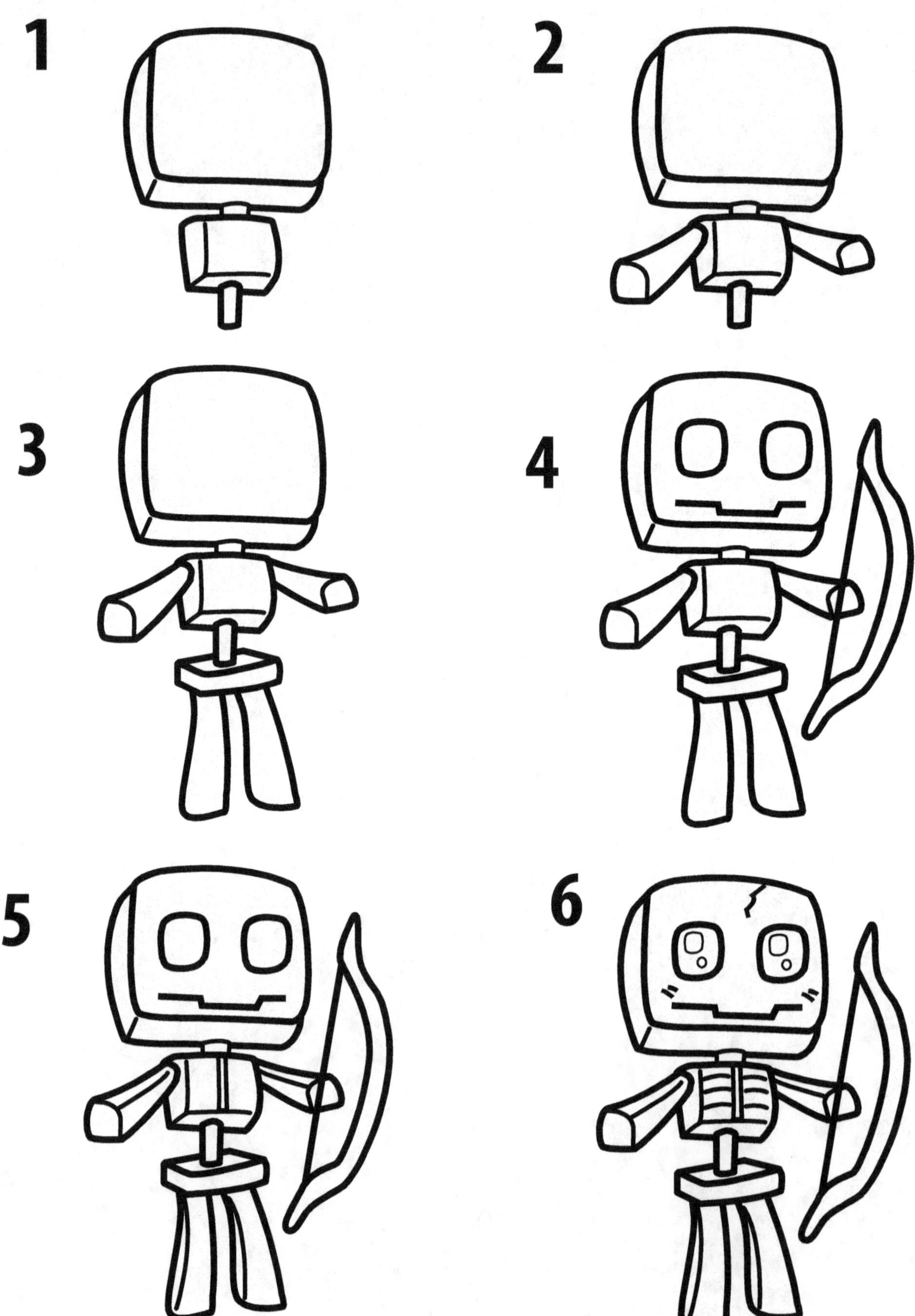

Now, it's your turn

Now, it's your turn

STEVE
1 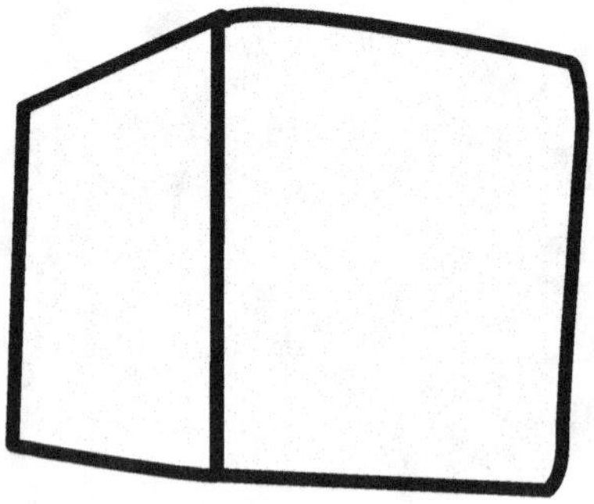
2 
3 
4 
5 
6

Now, it's your turn

ALEX

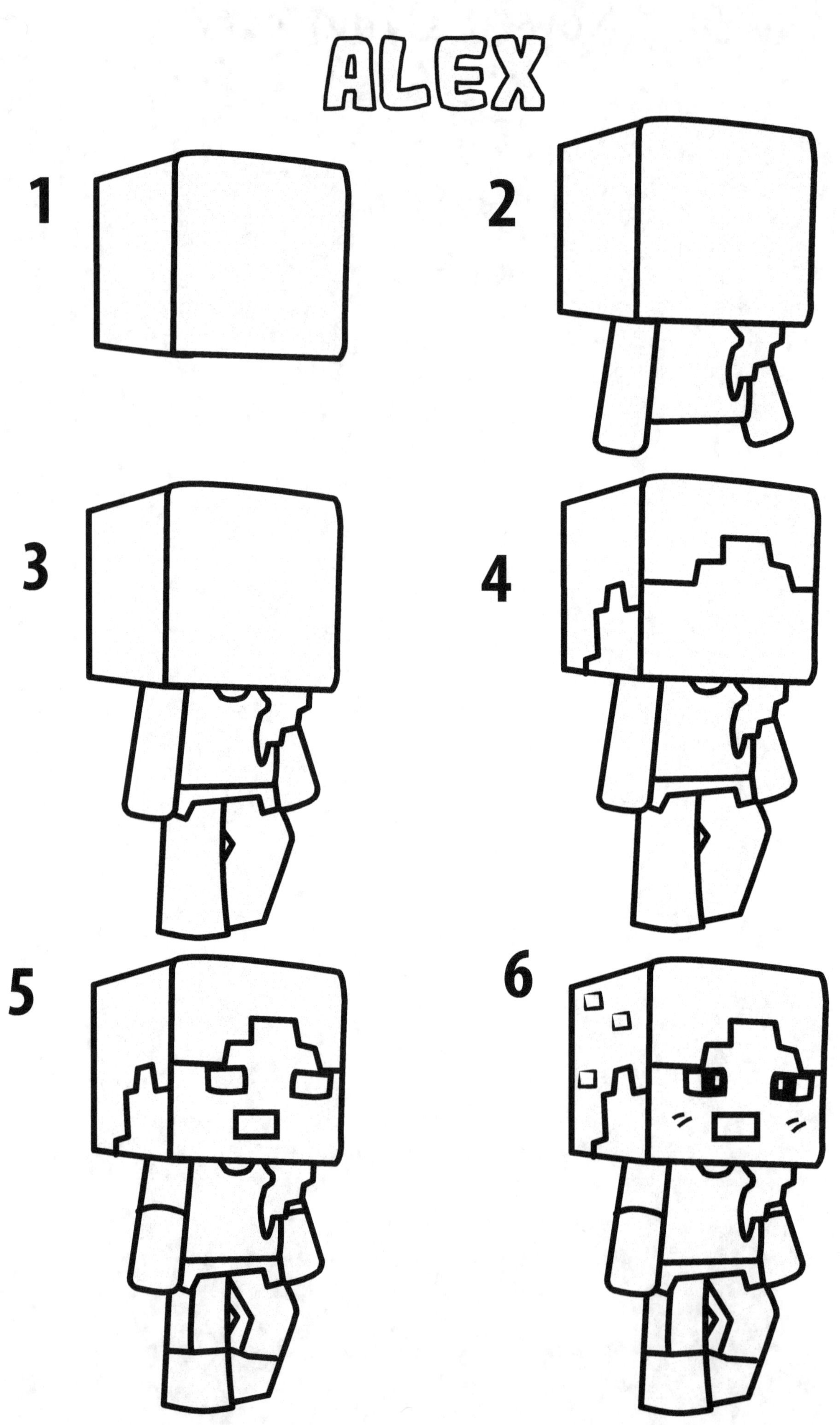

Now, it's your turn

ZOMBIE

Now, it's your turn

ENDERMAN

Now, it's your turn

WITCH

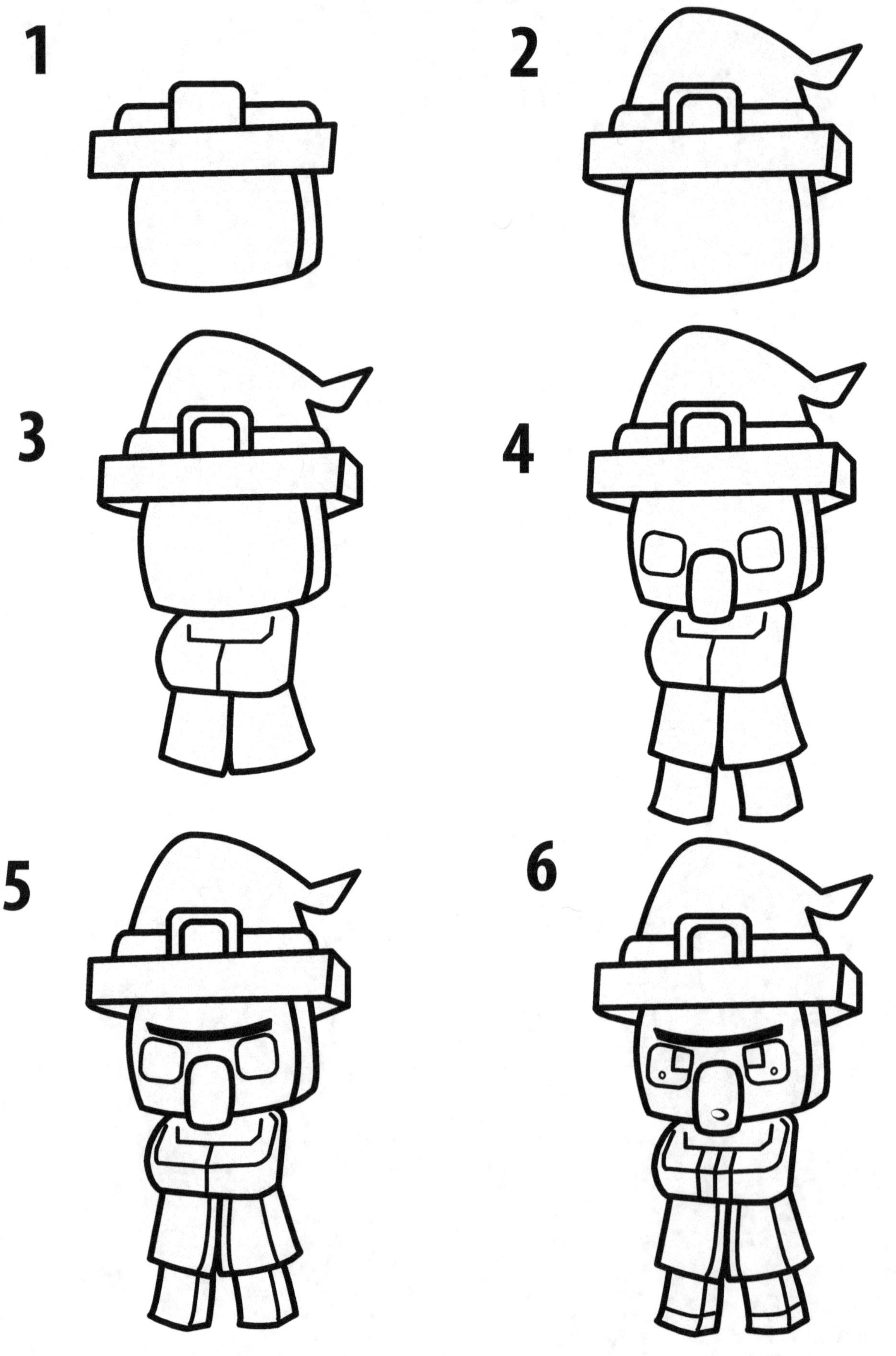

Now, it's your turn

WITHER

1

2

3

4

5

6

Now, it's your turn

GHAST

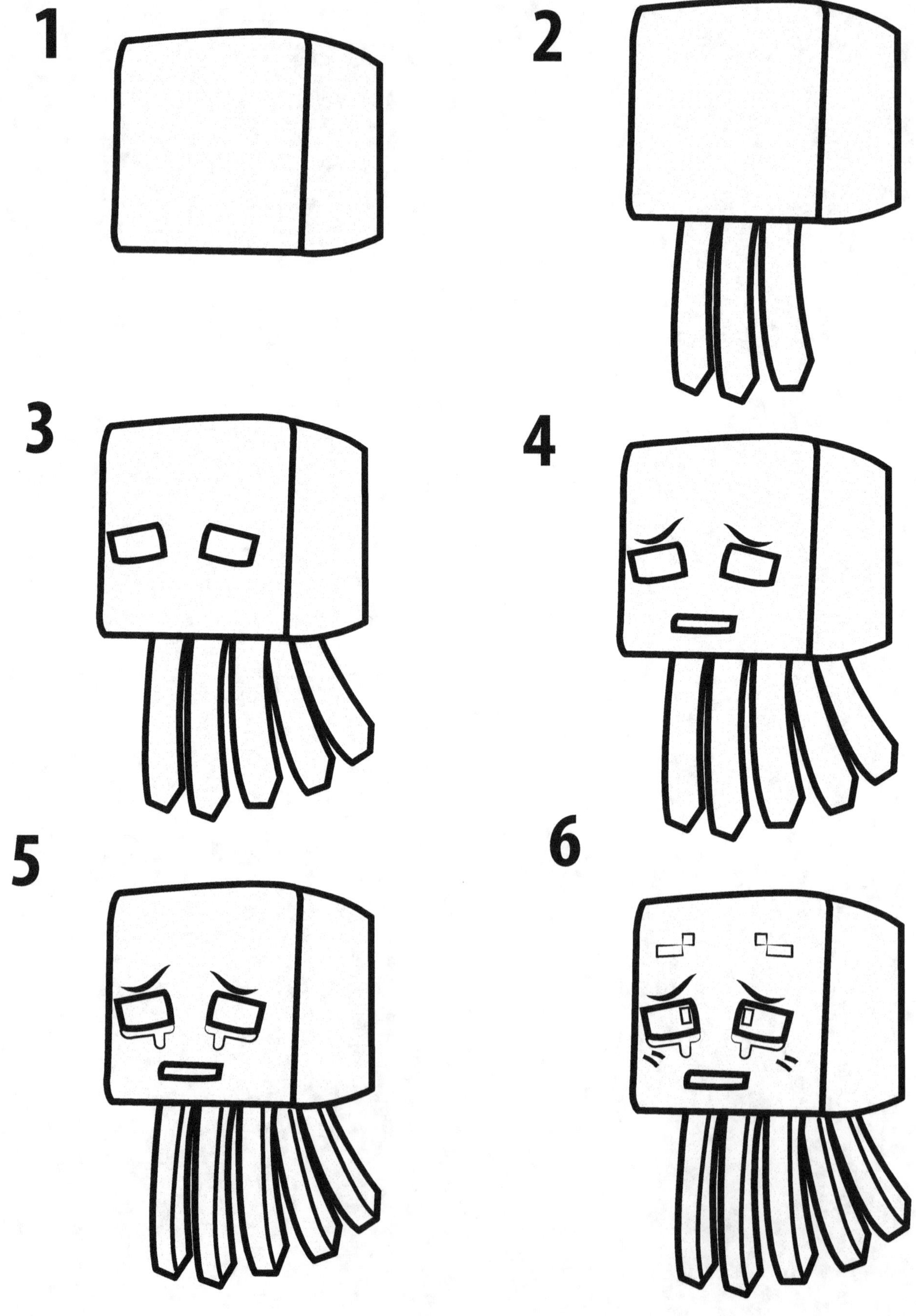

Now, it's your turn

CREEPER

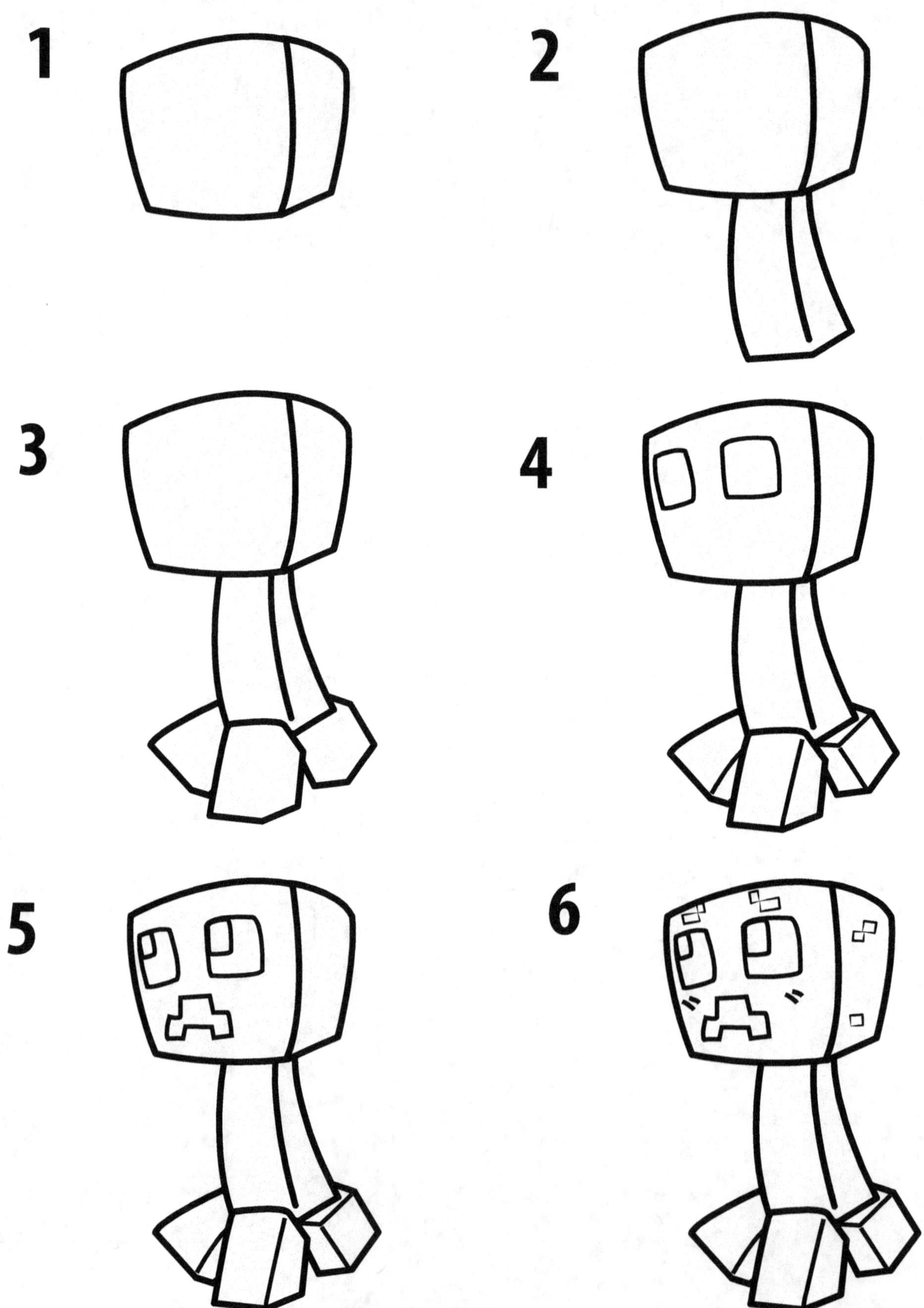

Now, it's your turn

SLIME

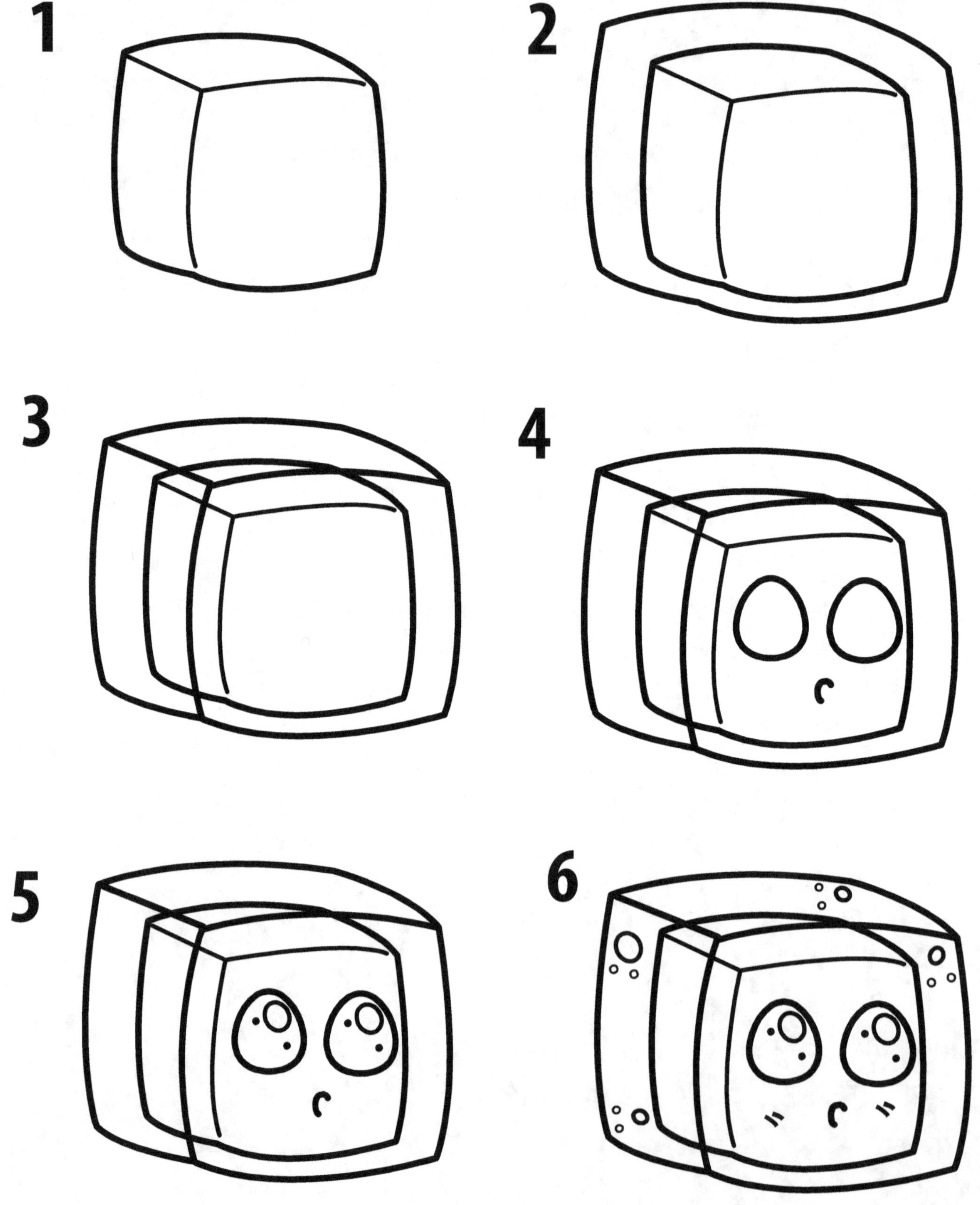

1

2

3

4

5

6

Now, it's your turn

BLAZE

Now, it's your turn

HOGLIN

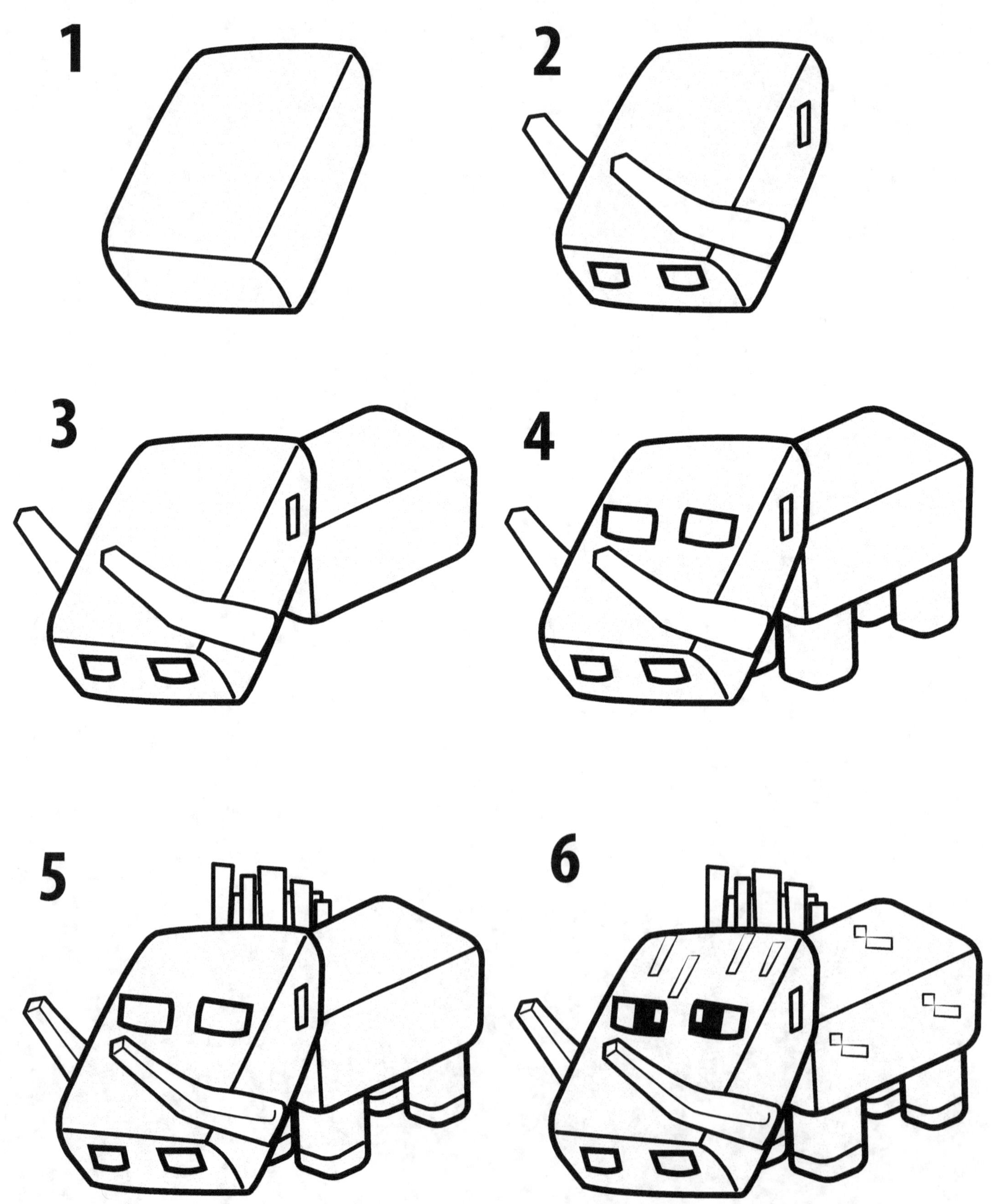

Now, it's your turn

PIGLIN

Now, it's your turn

GUARDIAN

Now, it's your turn

PHANTOM

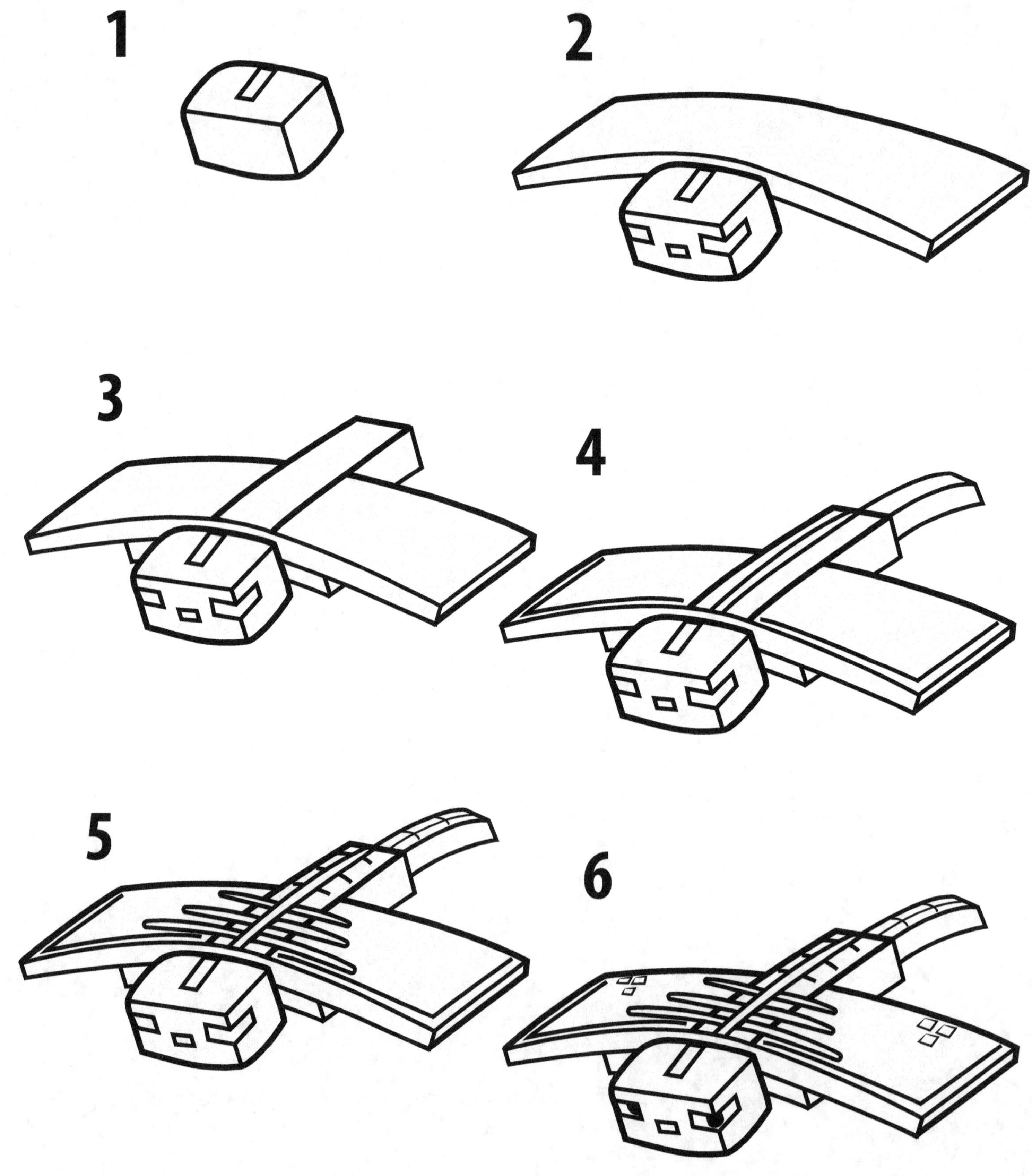

Now, it's your turn

MAGMA CUBE

Now, it's your turn

DROWNED

Now, it's your turn

SHULKER

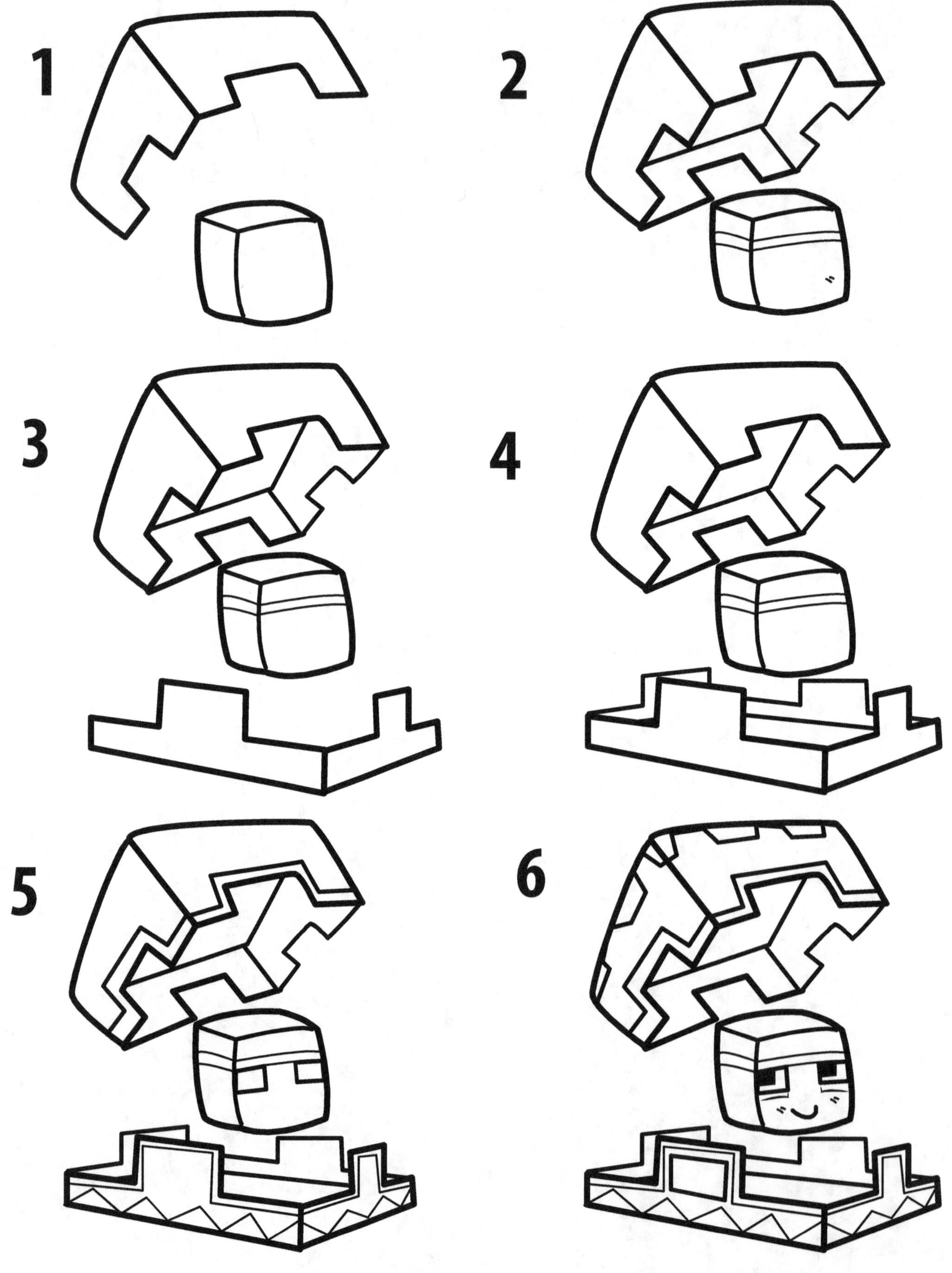

Now, it's your turn

SILVERFISH

Now, it's your turn

SNOW GOLEM

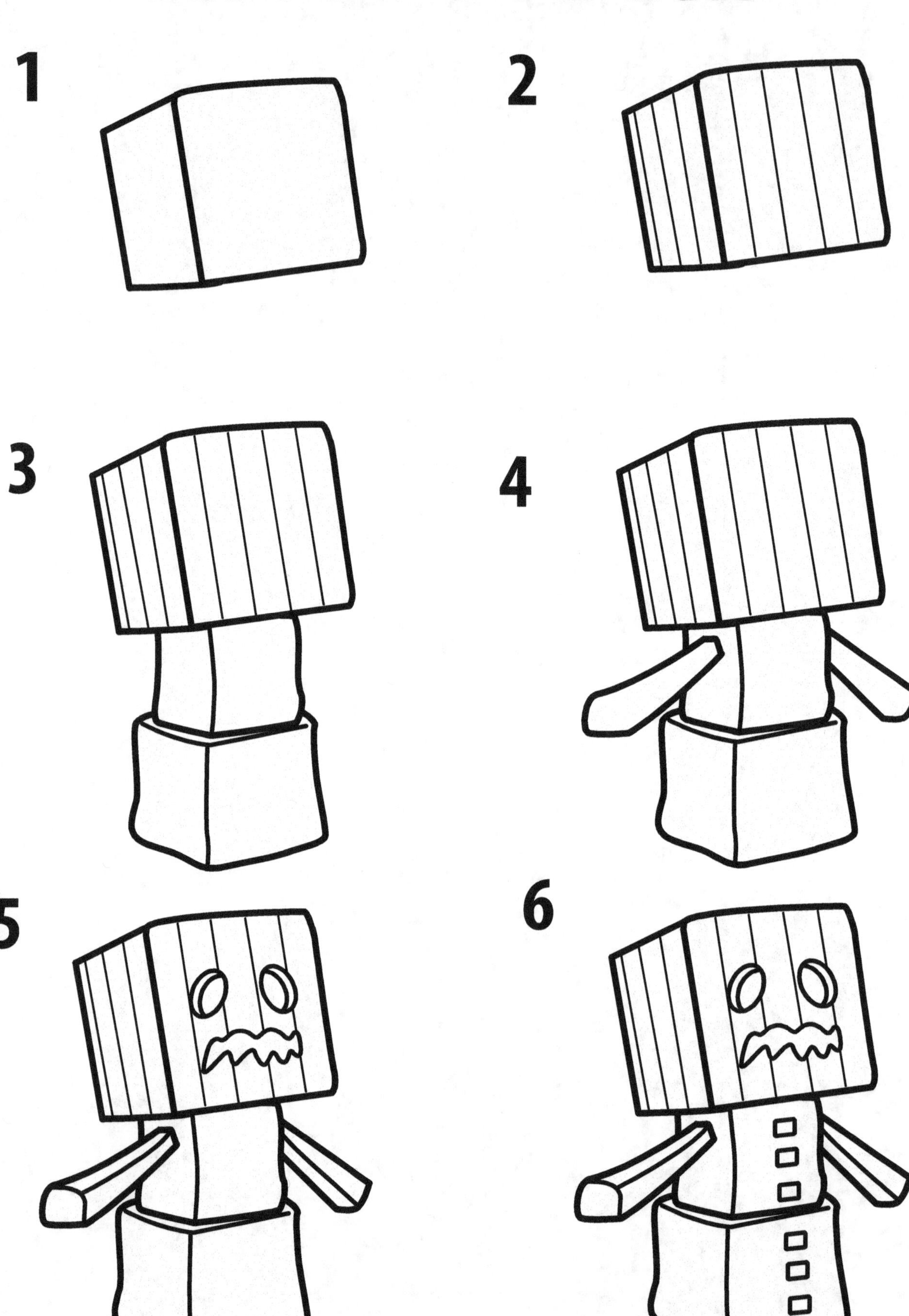

Now, it's your turn

IRON GOLEM

1

2

3

4

5

6

Now, it's your turn

ZOMBIE PIGMAN

Now, it's your turn

GLOW SQUID

Now, it's your turn

CHICKEN

Now, it's your turn

PIG

1

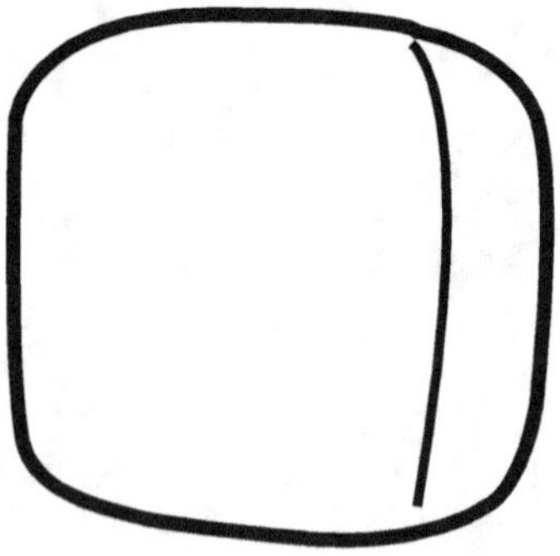

2

3

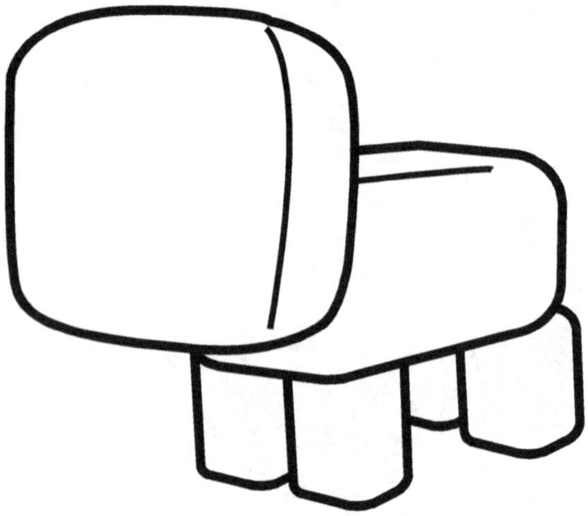

4

5

6

Now, it's your turn

Now, it's your turn

COW

Now, it's your turn

TURTLE

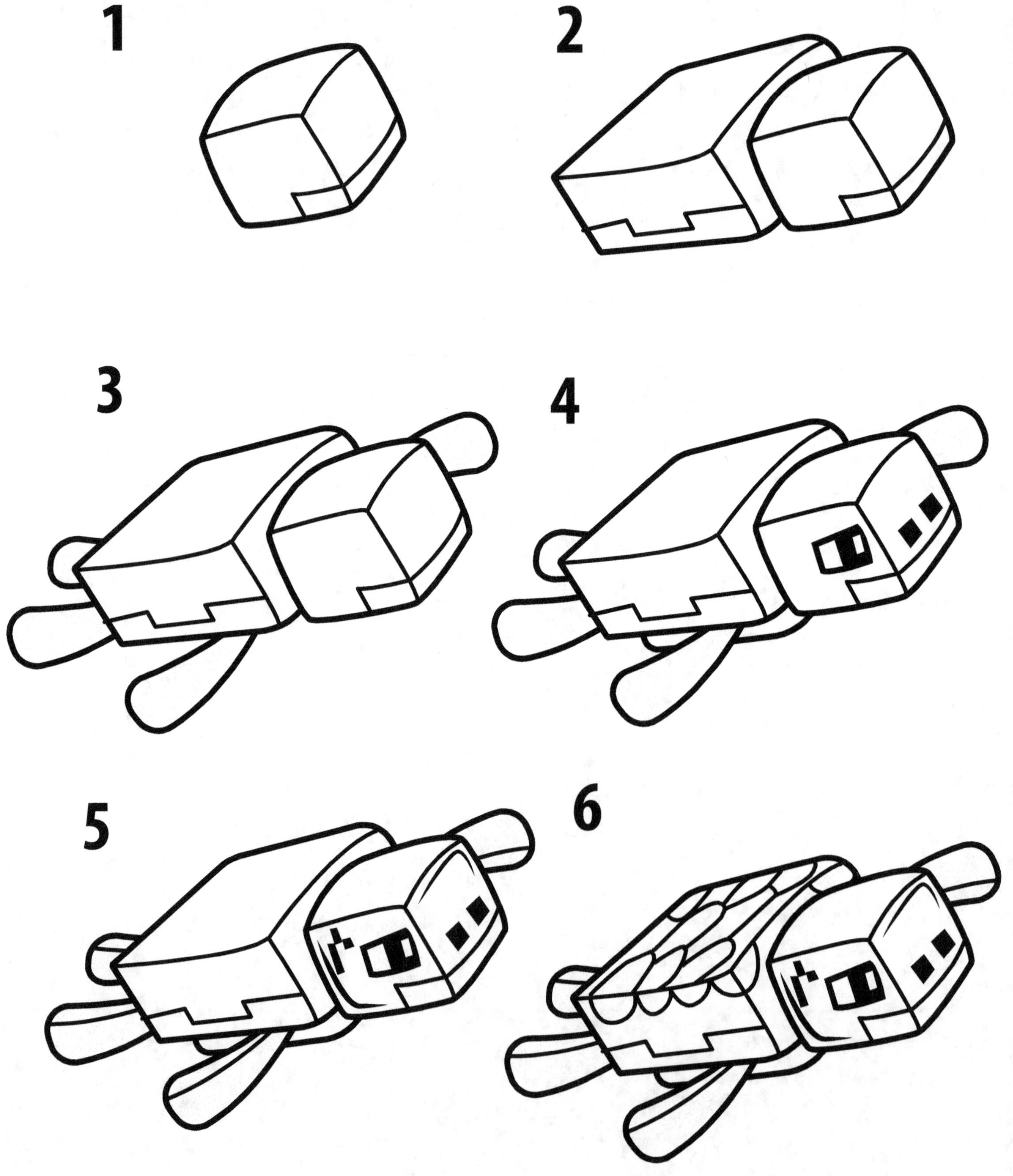

Now, it's your turn

DOLPHIN

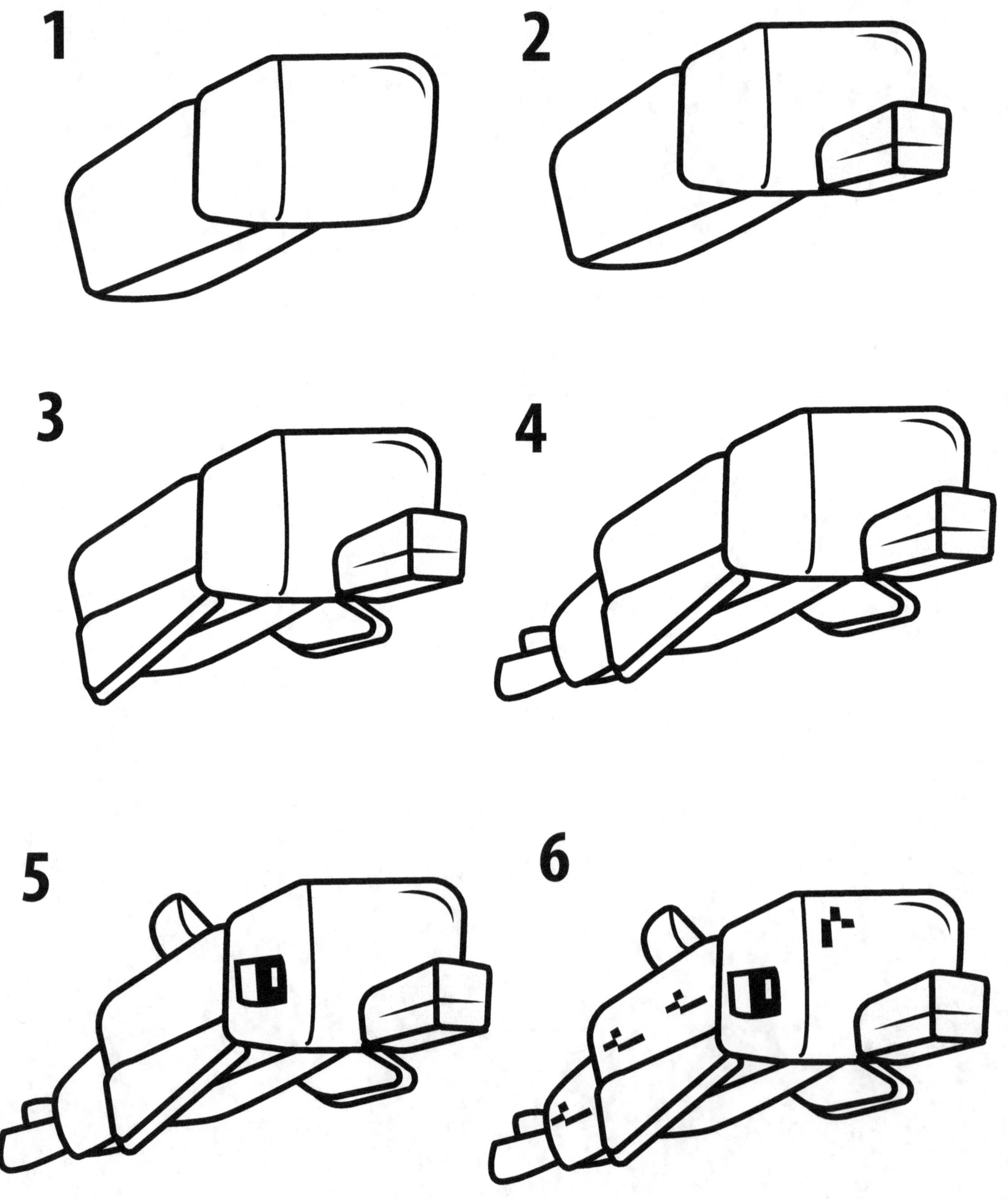

Now, it's your turn

AXOLOTL

Now, it's your turn

POLAR BEAR

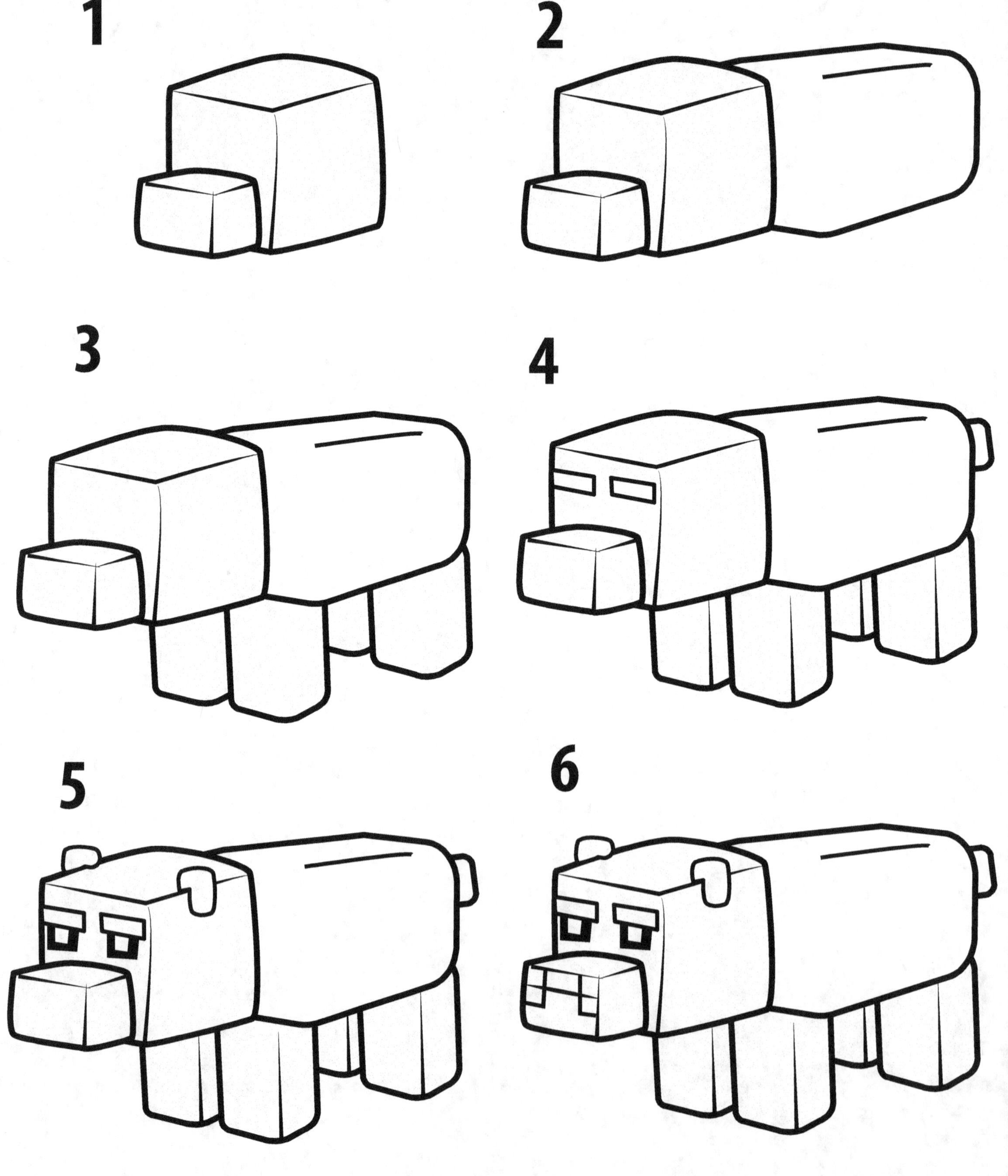

Now, it's your turn

OCELOT

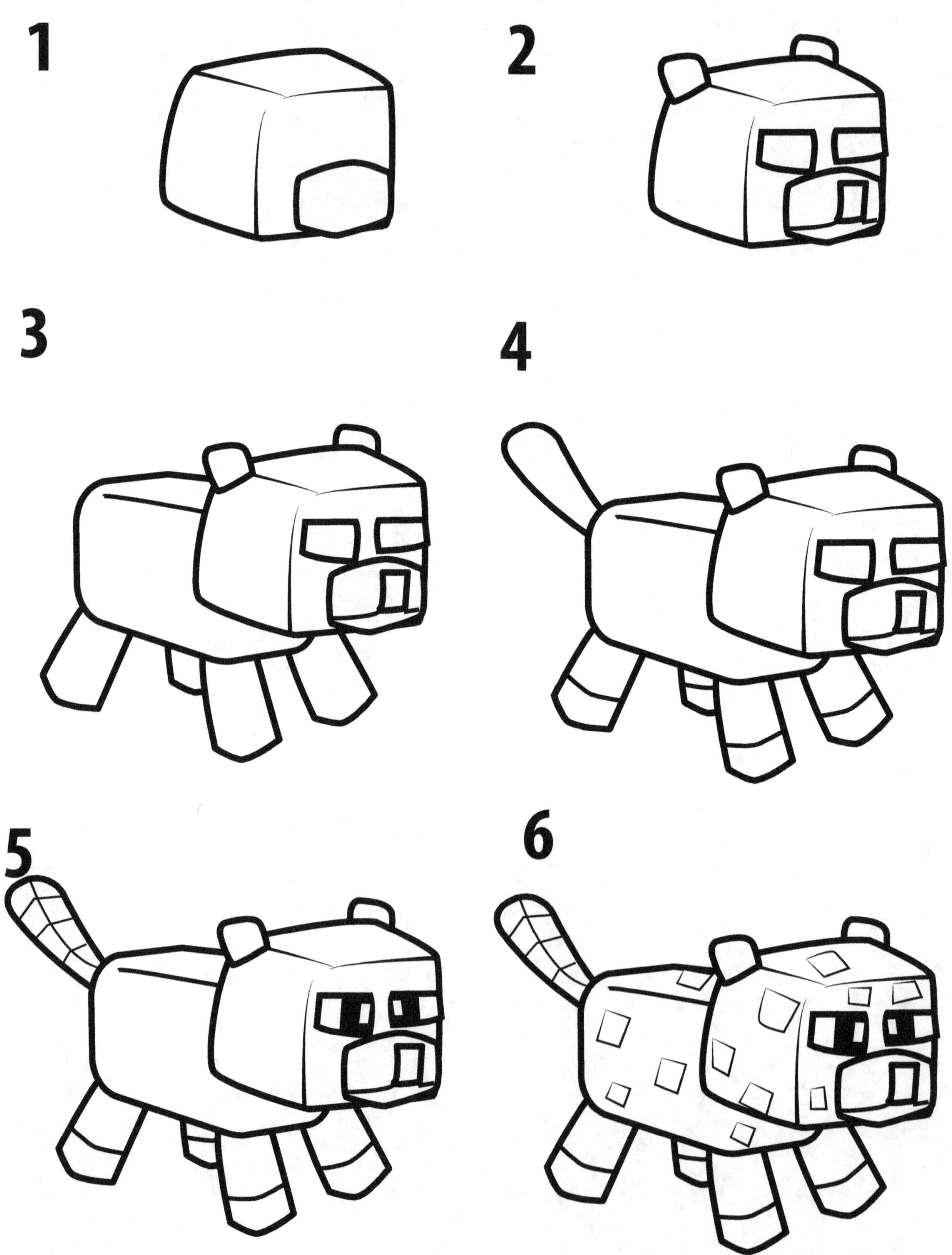

Now, it's your turn

ILAMA

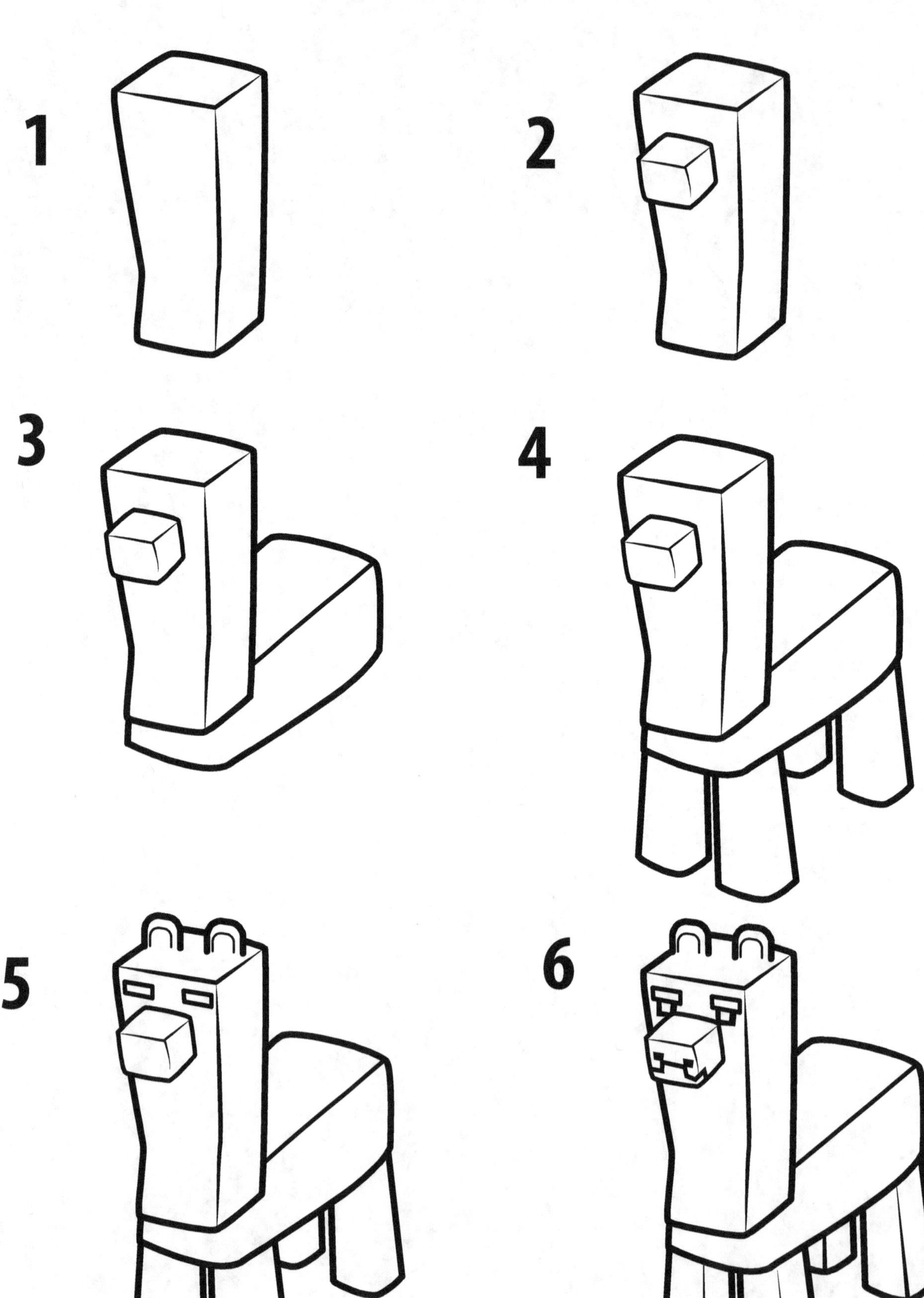

Now, it's your turn

Now, it's your turn

PARROT

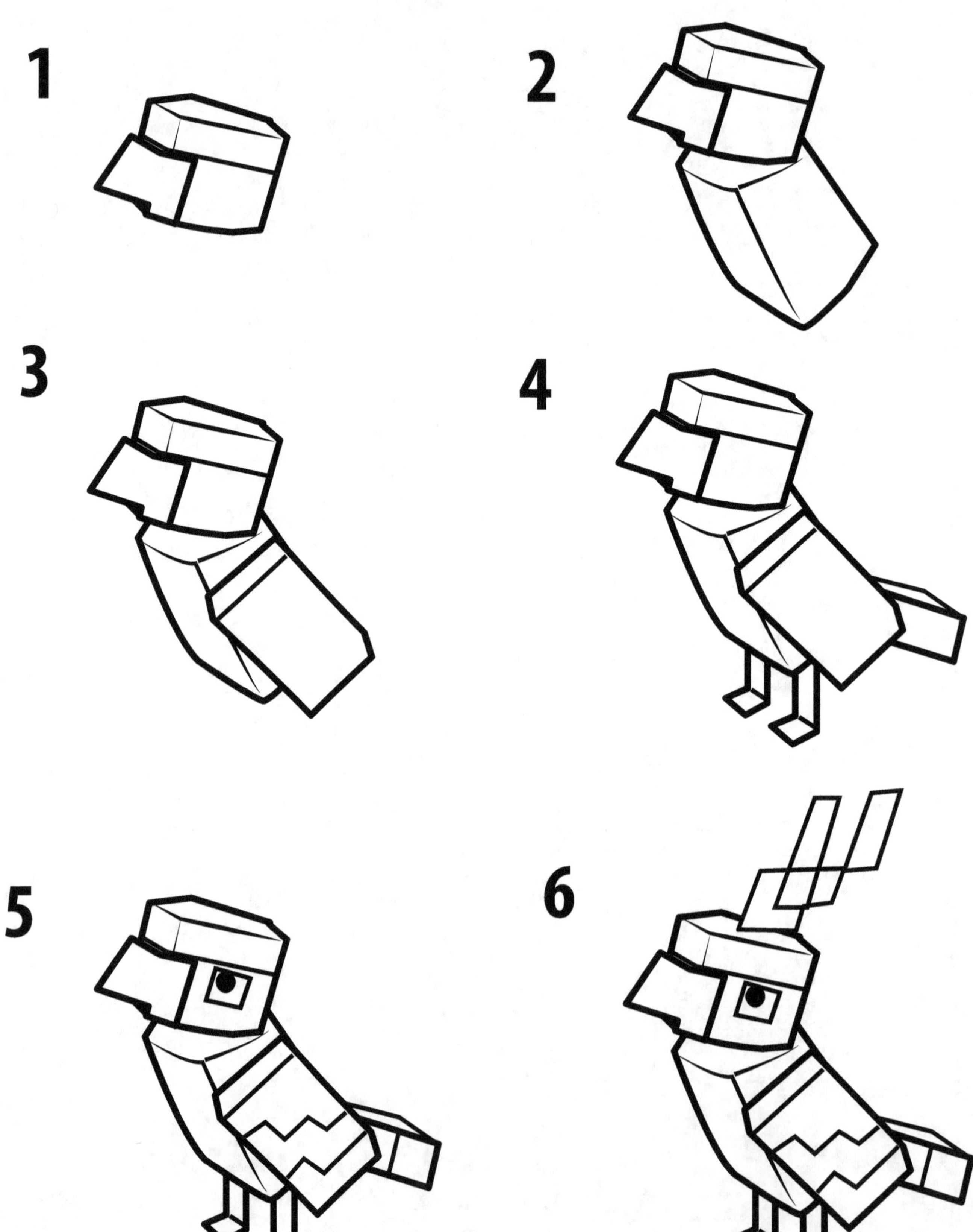

Now, it's your turn

SHEEP

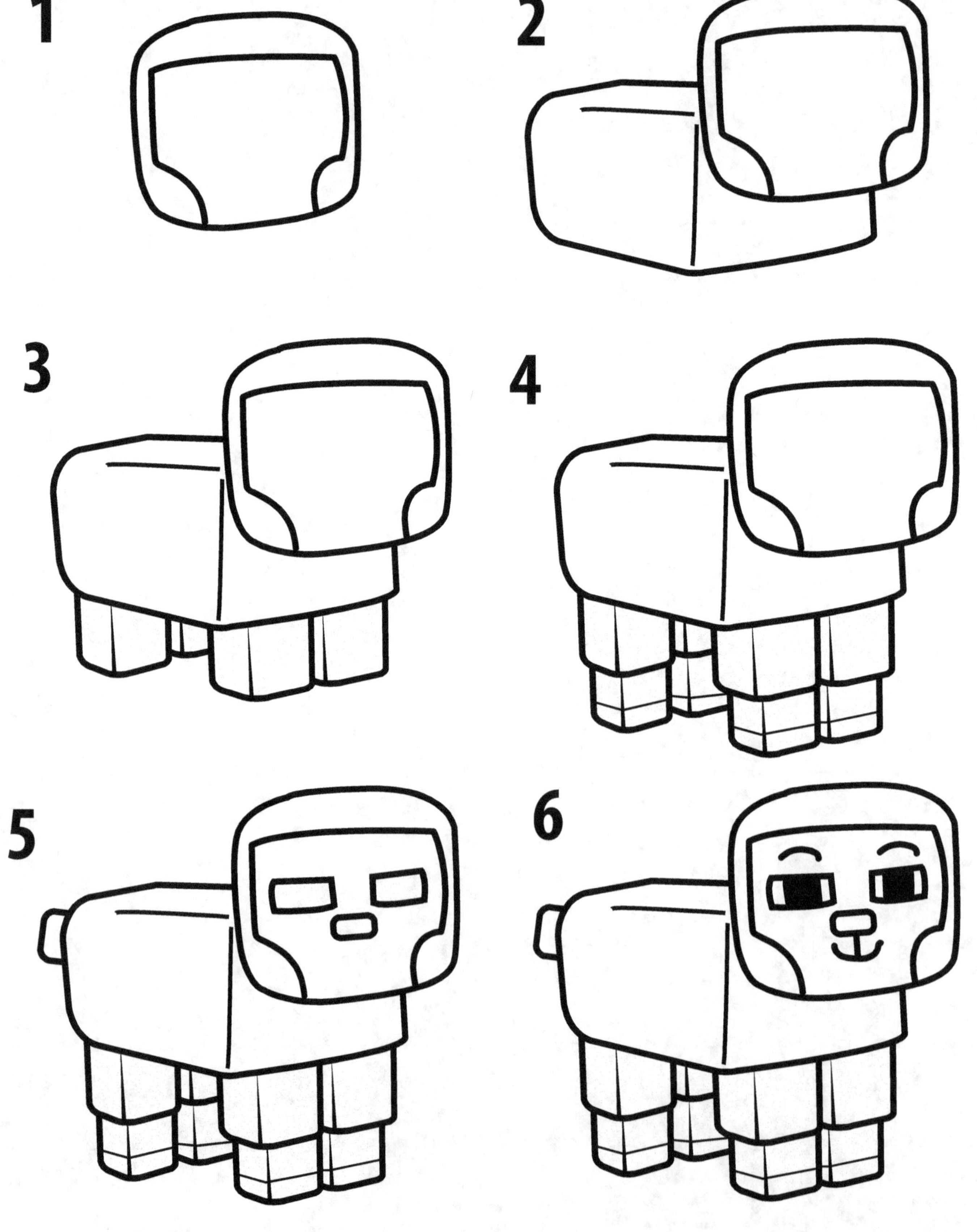

1

2

3

4

5

6

Now, it's your turn

WOLF

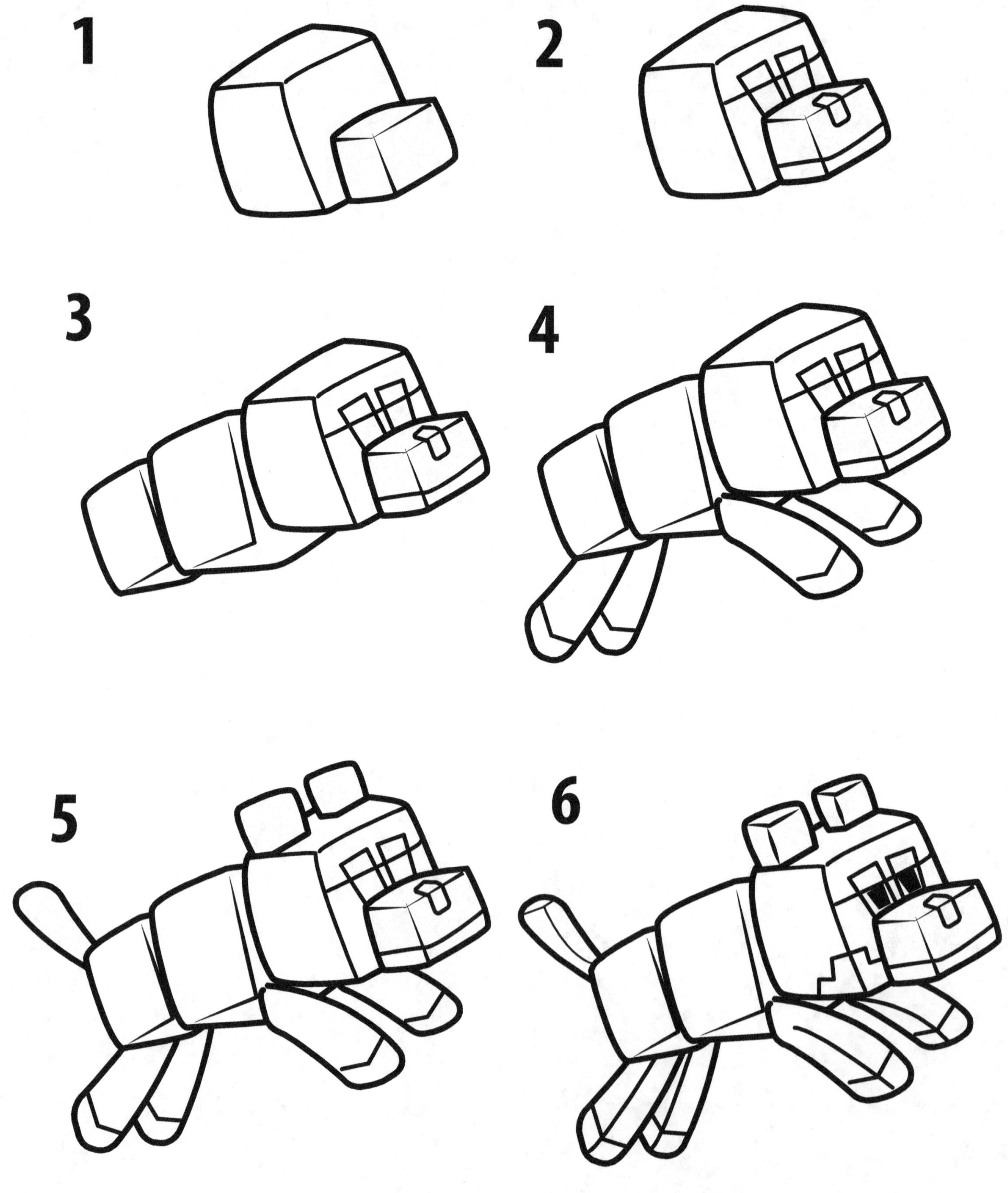

1

2

3

4

5

6

Now, it's your turn

CAT

1

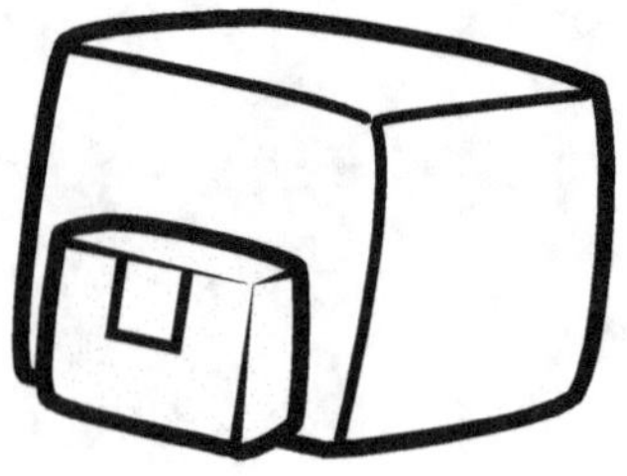

2

3

4

5

6

Now, it's your turn

HORSE

Now, it's your turn

DONKEY

Now, it's your turn

PANDA

1

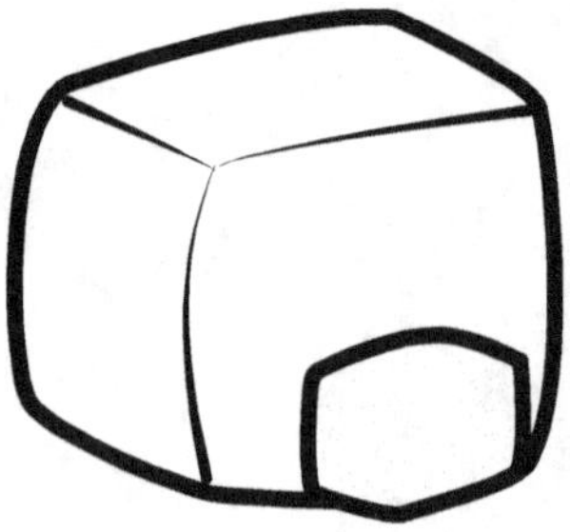

2

3

4

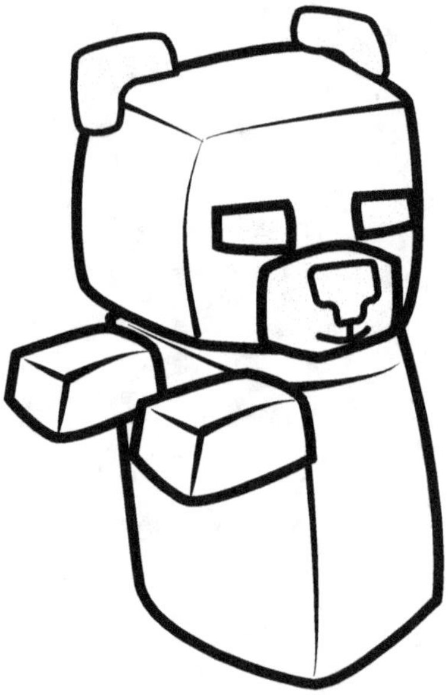

5

6

Now, it's your turn

STRAY

1

2

3

4

5

6

Now, it's your turn

VEX

1

2

3

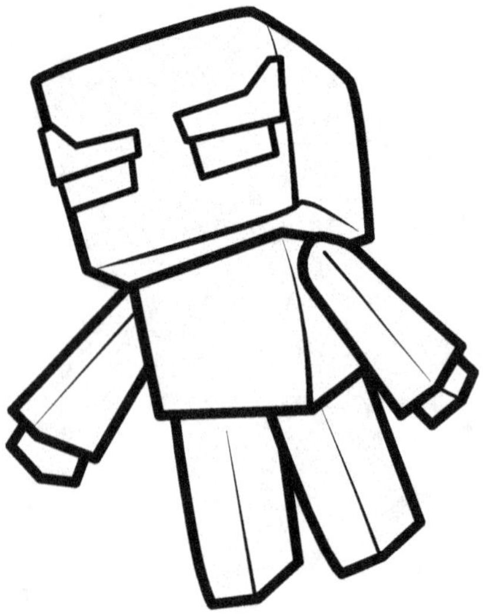

4

5

6

Now, it's your turn

HUSK

1

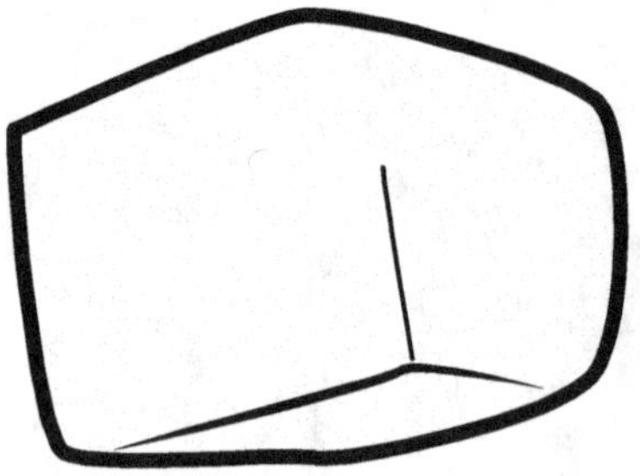

2

3

4

5

6

Now, it's your turn

Now, it's your turn

WANDERING TRADER

Now, it's your turn

PILLAGER

Now, it's your turn

VINDICATOR

1

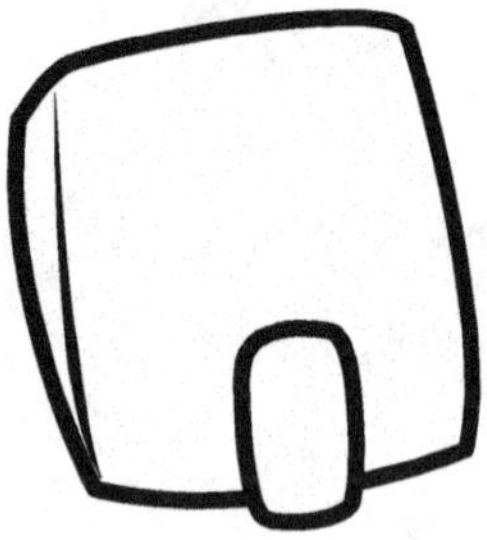

2

3

4

5

6

Now, it's your turn

EVOKER

1

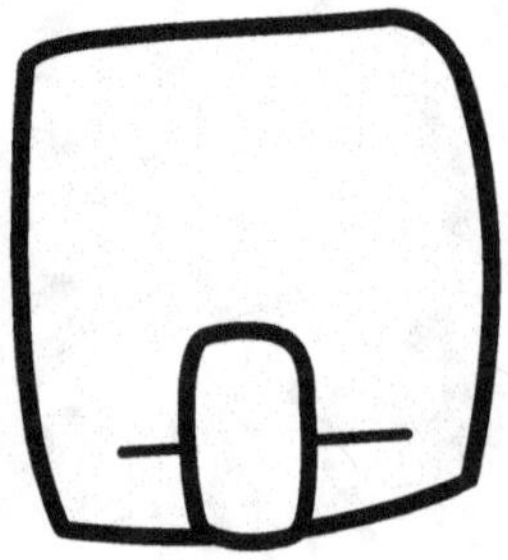

2

3

4

5

6

Now, it's your turn

VILLAGER

1

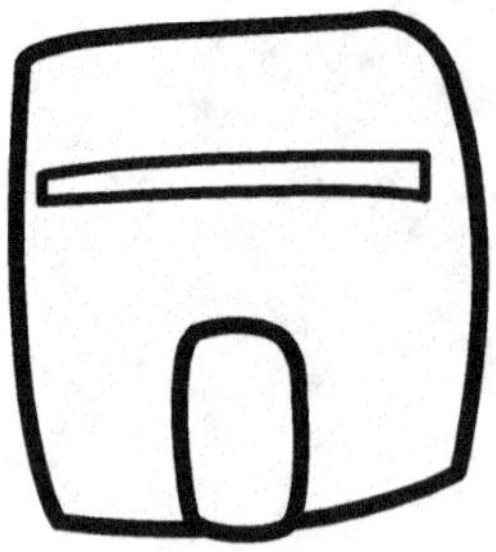

2

3

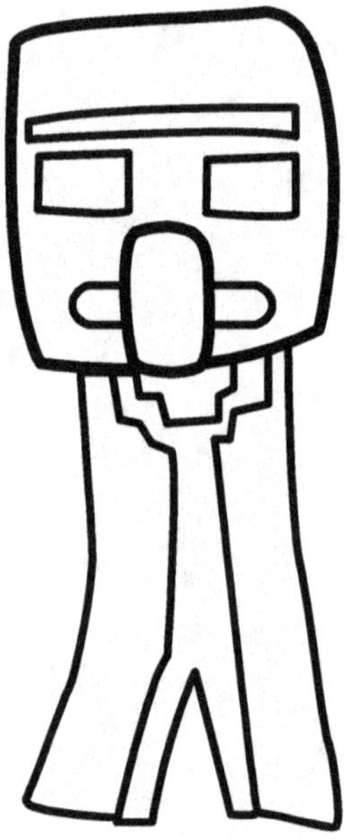

4

5

6

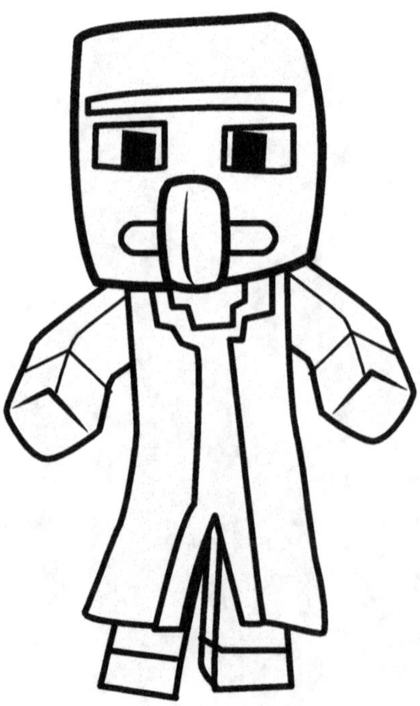

Now, it's your turn

TNT

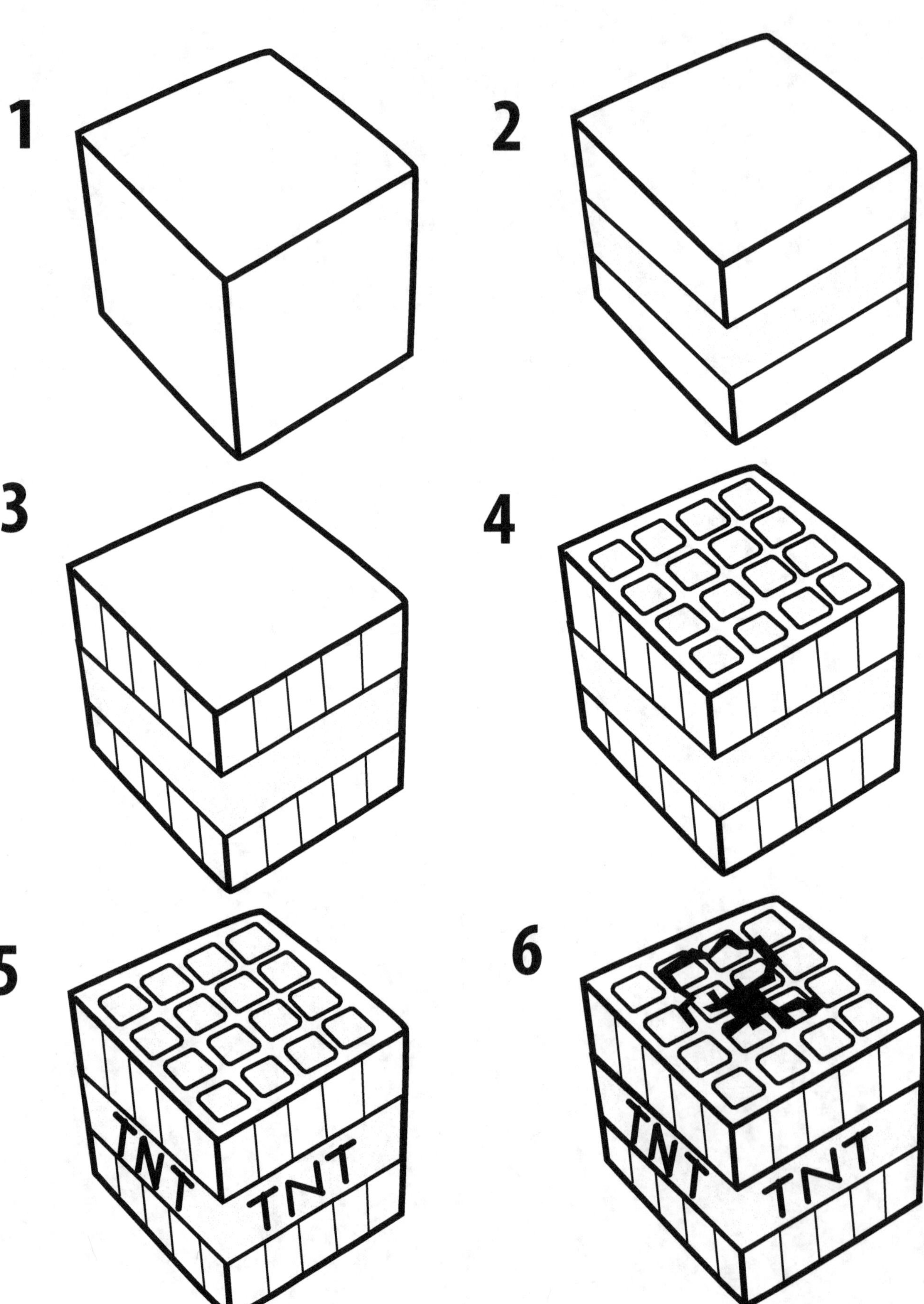

Now, it's your turn

DOWNLOAD 50
FREE COLORING PAGES

Visit our website or message to us!